SEF

IN STONES

SERMONS
IN STONES

BRIAN THOMPSON

Published by Brian Thompson

A CIP catalogue record for this book is available from the British Library.

ISBN 978-1-7398902-0-9

Book layout and cover design by Clare Brayshaw

Cover image Photo 79441364 © Muzzyco I Dreamstime.com

Prepared and printed by:

York Publishing Services Ltd
64 Hallfield Road
Layerthorpe
York YO31 7ZQ

Tel: 01904 431213

Website: www.yps-publishing.co.uk

To Martin and Liz,
two Knutsford friends whom I number amongst
my "encouragers" because they give me lots of
support and hope.

CONTENTS

ABOUT THE AUTHOR

Brian Thompson is a Methodist Local Preacher in the Alderley Edge and Knutsford Circuit. He moved to Knutsford in 2018 from Leeds having lived in the city from his birth in 1935. His first ventures into preaching came after returning from National Service in 1956.

His Recognition Service after preacher training came in 1962 in his Leeds (Armley) Circuit, now named Leeds South and West. His professional career was in teaching. Brian was a circuit tutor for some 15 years on the Methodist Faith and Worship Course for local preachers. He stepped down from this role when the new course was introduced.

Brian and Patricia were married in 1959: a very happy union of over 55 years producing 3 children and 5 grandchildren. His family are happily settled in Knutsford, Leicester and London.

AUTHOR'S PREFACE

"Sermons in Stones" is the title of a small book of sermons I have been working on over the summer. It is borrowed from Shakespeare's play "As You Like It" where in the first scene of the second act we hear these words from an exiled duke:

"Sweet are the uses of adversity,
Which like the toad, ugly and venomous,
Wears yet a precious jewel in his head:
And this our life, exempt from public haunt,
Finds tongues in trees, books in the
running brooks,
Sermons in stones,
and good in everything."

Reading those words leads me to ponder on the difficulties we have all had to face during the Covid Pandemic when this, our adversity, has caused us, in varying degrees, to be "exempted from public haunt." Our freedoms were restricted, our leisure activities reduced, we missed seeing our friends and family, sharing hugs, welcoming neighbours into our homes – and we didn't like it did we?

Somehow or other most of us coped and indeed some people found with the Bard that there are sweet rewards to be discovered in the "uses of adversity." We became more aware of nature, we began to appreciate the beauty of birdsong and came to realise that trees and running streams, even rocks and stones all have something to say to us if only we will pause to look and listen.

"As you like it?" Reflecting on our Covid adversity we have to protest, "We did NOT like it!" Hopefully though there were some lessons we learned because Shakespeare's optimistic "good in everything" conclusion is preferable to the half-empty glass outlook on life adopted by some folk.

Our lockdowns would have been better described as "lockups" because for those like me, with underlying health conditions, they were rather like imprisonments. Often ingeniously people found things to do. I occupied my time writing sermons. That kept this old, rusting brain stimulated. Consequently I now have a pile of unpreached sermons which will probably not reach any pulpit. Maybe they are not good enough anyway but I leave that for others to judge. This book is your chance.

Some of my Knutsford friends suggested a couple of years ago that I should consider getting some of my writing published. I resisted of course but my encouragers were not to be put off. Attempts to produce a whole book of sermons failed so the project was laid to rest. Then came further lockdowns and I toyed with the idea that maybe a limited number of sermons from that period could be circulated. That's what this is, and my hope and prayer is that at least some of my readers might find help and inspiration from my rambling thoughts.

Brian Thompson
Knutsford August 2021

NOW AND THEN

During the peak of the Covid-19 crisis I was asked two difficult questions within the space of a few days, both by e-mail. The first, from a Christian friend in North Yorkshire was "Do you think God has a plan in all this?"

The second was on similar lines but required a bit more thought because it was in an open e-mail to the members of a Philosophy Group. Dave is the leader and an atheist, as are a few of the others – all lovely people whose thinking and caring I deeply respect. He was throwing down the gauntlet when he asked, "Brian, are there any theological implications to be gleaned from this plague which has descended upon us?"

The first question, about the possibility of a divine plan, I could deal with in a couple of sentences, but the second, especially as it was in an open, to-be-shared response, took some research. To the first I could simply give a reply from my own reflections after years of reading and thinking, teaching and preaching. The second response required me to add that other Christians might come up with differing conclusions, depending mainly on their particular beliefs about the Bible – and from that, about the nature of God. As in many moral dilemmas of our day there can be no single

Christian answer. This diversity is part of our richness and provides opportunities for us to agree to disagree, and yet to obey Christ's command to "Love one another, so that the world might see and believe" (John 13.34-35) – thus enabling us to sing, with only the glimmer of a smile, Charles Wesley's inspiring words:

> *"Even now we think and speak the same,*
> *and cordially agree;*
> *concentred all through Jesu's name,*
> *in perfect harmony" (STF 608)*

OK! Maybe a slight stretch of the imagination is sometimes required!

But I have jumped right in at the deep end haven't I and that's not a good way to start any sermon. So before you turn off let's go simple. Why have I given this talk the title "Now and Then"?

Well, from cradle to grave, we all get asked questions: questions from the simple to the profound, from the casual information-seeking to the deliberately pointed, maybe conveying a hidden judgement, requiring a careful answer and perhaps an answer which tries to hide the fact that actually we weren't really listening anyway. (And we are all guilty of that at times – are we not?)

Some questions ask us "Do you ever..?" They can begin early in life: Do you ever wash behind your ears? Do you ever comb your hair? (our PM missed that last one and nobody asks me that question because there is not much left to comb!) Do you ever do your homework on the bus on your way to school?

As I get older my handwriting gets worse. It's always been too small anyway but I still remember an embarrassing moment in class when Mr Marshall, the Maths teacher, returned some homework with the question, in a loud voice, "Thompson, do you spend the weekends writing the Lord's Prayer on a sixpence?"

I had a further lesson years later when roles were reversed and I returned an essay to a pupil on which I had written the comment "I cannot read your writing". The boy came back to me at the end of the lesson asking "What does this say sir. I can't make it out?"

Other uncomfortable questions I could face are

"Do you ever watch "Neighbours?""

"Do you ever sing solos in church?"

"Now and then" could be my response to both questions (although to the solo one perhaps it should now be – not any more!)

Questions for *you* though: "Do you ever tell your wife that you love her, buy her a bunch of red roses?" (Perhaps you should. Start tomorrow.) "Do you ever take breakfast in bed to your husband?"

And a question for all of us: "Do you ever fall asleep during the sermon?" Is it now and then?

Perhaps you can't answer because you are already asleep! "Do you ever wear a tie in church?" "Now and then?"

Even St Paul used the words "now" and "then". They are permissible, even when they reveal our attempt (politician like) to avoid a direct, full and honest answer. When did Paul use these two words together? I could say "Now and then" but certainly once and the evidence is in the famous reading from 1 Corinthians 13.

Now I admit that I have cheated by going off at a tangent because the context here is not that of asking or answering questions. The Apostle's words and message here though were very important and very relevant for his listeners in the late 1st century and they are equally worth reading and thinking about today in our 21st century. ("At last!" you say. "He's arrived at his text and title!" of "Now and Then.")

After launching into his wonderful poem about Faith, and Hope, and Love, and before his forceful conclusion that we should make Love our aim in life, St Paul writes this:

> *"When I was a child I spoke like a child,*
> *I thought like a child, I reasoned like a child;*
> *when I became an adult, I put an end to*
> *childish ways. For* ***now*** *(for the present) we*
> *see in a mirror, dimly, but* ***then*** *(after death)*
> *we will see face to face. Now (in this world)*
> *I know only in part,* ***then*** *(beyond this life) I*
> *will know fully, even as I have been fully*
> *known."*

So, to help us in our search for this "knowledge" we are told of three requisites – we must have faith, we require hope and above all we need love.

And if life is to be at all fulfilling we need to possess these three things NOW – not next week, not when we have achieved some goal or milestone in our lives, not in the some-time future, but NOW.

But where do we fit in, where does society stand, as we stagger out of a coronavirus pandemic, reeling?

Some of you will remember the old protest songs of the late 1950s and 60s when the world had been in fear of nuclear warfare. Young people especially wanted harmony and love as they sang "Where have all the Flowers Gone?" There was a strong determination that they would make the world a better place as they strummed their guitars and hammered out the message "The times they are a changing".

In many ways how true that prophecy has proved to be. Thanks to modern technology, scientific discovery, worldwide travel, the mass media, food production and distribution we would hardly recognise that post-war period were we to be teleported back. The speed of change has been truly phenomenal!

Why even the Church – not noted for change ("The wheels of God grind slowly" the saying goes) has seen many new forms of ministry and styles of worship. Though in some thinking we seem, and often are, a few miles behind the rest of society.

In many areas though we do point the ways ahead so let's not beat ourselves up too much.

In fact let's remember and boast that the Church has often been, and still is, at the very forefront of social reform and change. Examples reel off the tongue: caring for the sick, feeding the hungry, battling against the slave trade and apartheid, supporting the Trades

Union movement, being instrumental in free education for all, working for prison reform and improving children's factory conditions, and so on... We can rightly be proud of this part of the church's history – a glorious heritage – and of her ongoing outreach in modern times.

Why did opponents of the Early Church stand back in astonishment and comment "Look at these Christians. See how much they care!" and why does the Church today continue even more ingeniously to demonstrate such caring love?

Is it because the Church and Christianity's core aim and message is all about CHANGE?

We have just sung the words: "The church of Christ in every age, beset by change but Spirit led must claim and test its heritage and keep on rising from the dead."

Flick through the Gospels and you will detect this emphasis on the importance of change. Preachers might use different terms such as conversion, salvation, being born again, being transformed – all of which contain elements of meaning which are embraced by some but off-putting to others – but essentially they all involve change – change of life, change of heart, change of direction, change of meaning and of purpose.

At my previous church in Leeds we have a banner which replaces the Christmas ones. It simply says "All Things New". Actually it's not just a New Year message is it? It's for all the year and all the years.

In the opening chapter of Mark's gospel we are told that Jesus came into Galilee proclaiming the good news of God...saying "Repent and believe.."

Repent is not just to say sorry, it is to "Change your life" as the Message version puts it.

Consider John's gospel. Why does the author include an unlikely story of what he says is the first miracle that Jesus performed – that of water into wine at a wedding in Cana? Why is that followed by Jesus causing chaos in the Jerusalem Temple overturning the tables of the money changers and traders and driving them out with a whip? That incident is at the climax of Jesus's ministry in the other gospels but John places it right at the start of his story. Why? What statement is the author making about Jesus? Does he want his readers to understand that here, in Jesus, is One who changes things?

Jesus challenges the orthodox Jewish religion of his day exemplified in the Temple system of worship through animal sacrificing. He has opened the way for us to "worship the Father in spirit and in truth" as he explained to the Samaritan woman at the well (John 4 v.23-24).

Moving on to the wedding feast and the miracle of water into wine. William Barclay's comment, as long ago as 1955 is worth quoting in full:

"In this story John is saying that when the grace of Jesus comes to people, there is enough and to spare, for all. No wedding party on earth could drink one hundred and eighty gallons of wine and no need on earth can exhaust the grace of Christ. There is a glorious superabundance in the grace of Christ. John is telling us that in Jesus the imperfections have become perfection, and the

grace has become illimitable, sufficient and more than sufficient for every need."

"I am come that you may have life, real and eternal" Jesus says later (John 10 v.10), "more abundant than you could ever dream of." At the beginning of Mark's gospel, when Jesus says "Change your life" is this promise of abundant living what he is leading us up to: That if we aim at changing our lives he will add his grace to help us for he is a life changer and Christianity is all about change?

When I wrote my e-mails to my two friends about where I thought God was in this pandemic I gave my opinion that God was not in there with a plan to test us or to punish us for our sins; that the idea of God being a cruel, stern judge and interventionalist is abhorrent to me and far removed from the picture of a loving and forgiving God presented to us by Jesus. At the same time, I concluded, perhaps God would be pleased at the amazing outpouring of love from people coming together in unity and the spirit of neighbourliness. That would seem to be part of the divine mind from the very beginning – as those meaningful creation myths of Genesis suggest.

Actually all this has been the role and the message of the Church for society and the world before the coronavirus struck. This means that we don't have to change our message of good news to fit the developing aftermath situation, but we do have to reinforce it with increased confidence. This is a marvellous time of opportunity for Christians. We might have to change some attitudes and approaches but, praise God, the harvest is ripe, and in need of willing and enthusiastic workers.

To my regret I was not taught Latin at school but we all pick up Latin words and phrases. One of my favourite sayings is "Carpe Diem" which means "seize the day, seize the moment". I suggest that the church could well make that our rallying call, our motto; "Carpe Diem!"

My personal hope for the worldwide Church is that as a result of our experiences of dealing with Covid-19 we will see local churches and individual Christians who are more open to new ways of thinking outside of our usual boxes when we consider church doctrines and practices.

Two areas in particular concern me. You may well disagree with mine and you will have your own suggestions.

I would look for more openness towards other Faiths with the recognition that the truth about God is not confined to Christianity and that there are ways in which we can and must work together. We are after all united in demonstrating the importance of spiritual values, worship, loving our neighbours, caring for our precious, beautiful and fragile environment.

Secondly I would look for an openness towards any issues which society has come to terms with but which many Christians would dismiss, without consideration, such as our attitude to LGBTQ+ rights. There is a place for doubt in our faith, famously referred to as a "cloud of unknowing". You would think that Doubt is the opposite of Faith but there is a school of thought that the opposite of Faith is Certainty. If you are dead certain about some belief or practice then you could be closing your mind to the consideration of wider views.

In the recent lockdown some American Pastors tried to keep their churches open for services. One lady declared to a TV interviewer: "God will keep us safe because we are preserved by the blood of Jesus!" That is a closed mind mentality which is disturbingly bonkers.

The older I get the less certain I become about some of our Church beliefs and practices but I welcome not knowing because it is through grappling with uncertainty that our faith grows.

Of some things we are convinced and can say so, but generally speaking an open minded approach may be preferable.

Those are my hopes for the Church of the future – open hearts to welcome all, open minds to embrace new challenges and ideas.

The question being asked across the world is "When this pandemic is over will we return to normal – or will a new normal emerge fostered by the spirit of love and co-operation with a desire to work for a better world?"

That same thinking will include the Church. We too will have to make changes, humbly and prayerfully. Who knows what the Church will be like in say 20, 50 or 100 years' time? Post coronavirus this church here may begin to look different, but let us seize the moment – "Carpe Diem". The challenge is exciting, and we are part of it.

You will notice that I have only dealt with the NOW of St Paul's NOW and THEN and you will be glad that I do not intend to say anything much about the THEN, apart from pointing out that when the Apostle writes to the Roman Christians about the THEN state of life after death he goes into his conviction mode, which is why the Romans 8 passage is often read at funerals.

"I am convinced," he thunders, "that nothing, not even death can separate us from God's love for us in Jesus Christ."

Charles Wesley shared Paul's optimism and his hope when he wrote his confident hymn "Love Divine" especially in the last verse: We shall be

"Changed from glory into glory;" (note it is a gradual process through life)

"Till in heaven we take our place!" (which is our THEN)

"Till we cast our crowns before thee

Lost in wonder, love and praise."

To that we can surely add a loud AMEN!...AMEN!!

(Author's footnote: it is obvious that there is far too much material for one sermon here. This often happens and it becomes necessary to do some drastic pruning before a final draft is reached. If "Now and Then" were ever to get preached a lot of work would have to first take place.)

A PILGRIM'S PROGRESS

It is said that in Victorian England the only book, apart from the Bible, which children were allowed to read on Sunday was John Bunyan's "The Pilgrim's Progress". This strict attitude to the Sabbath was amusingly highlighted in a film I watched during our enforced Covid-19 lockdown. The stay at home policy had at least some compensations!

Whiskey Galore is set in the 1940s in a remote Scottish island where the rule of the Kirk was very strong. A large boat with a cargo of barrels of whiskey gets stranded on the rocks in stormy seas. It so happened that all the whiskey in the island's pub and shop had long since been consumed so the shipwreck, in which no one was killed or injured, was seen as a godsend. The weekend was fast approaching but the islanders had just time to unload the precious cargo into the entrance of a cave before any excise men appeared to claim the whiskey. But it was not sufficiently hidden to escape any inquisitive stranger bent on finding it. The trouble came when the bell for the Sabbath rang out from the church and immediately the dozen or so busy workers turned back from the beach, hurrying home to change into Sunday suits and go to the Kirk service. All work ceased on the Sabbath, even rescuing shipwrecked booty. When the bell for the end of the Sabbath sounded there followed another quick change and off they all scurried back down to the beach. Maybe some of the islanders put away their Bibles and copies of The Pilgrim's Progress for the next six days.

Even if you have never read John Bunyan's book you will probably know that it is an allegory as much as an adventure story in which every part points us to the challenges and struggles of the Christian faith. Much of it was written in a prison cell. It's in two parts, the first being published in 1678. It has been described as one of the most significant works of religious theological fiction in English literature. Its full title is "The Pilgrim's Progress from this world to that which is to come." Translated into more than 200 languages it, like the Bible, has never been out of print.

It tells the story of Christian who sets off from his home in the City of destruction on a pilgrimage to find the Celestial City. All sorts of adventures are encountered on the way such as getting bogged down in the muddy Slough of Despond, arriving at the Wicket Gate which leads to the straight and narrow King's Highway, losing his burdensome backpack of sin at the hill of the cross, for it to roll away into an empty sepulchre.

The journey continues with further difficulties ahead: the Valley of the Shadow of Death, a city called Vanity Fair, offering all the tempting sins of worldly pleasure, battles with the frightening Giant Despair till at last the final river is crossed and the Celestial City is reached.

There are dozens of characters in "The Pilgrim's Progress" and as I mention a few you might find yourself thinking "Oh I recognise some of them!" Hopeful, Watchful, Faithful, Greatheart, Goodwill. All positive people, but what about Mr Despondency, Mr Feeble Mind, Mr Ready to Halt, Timorous, Talkative (what, me?) and worst of all, Hypocrisy?

Most Christians will regard themselves as pilgrims on a journey of faith and their source book is packed with pilgrimages both large and small, from Moses leading his people from slavery in Egypt to their Promised Land, to Jesus "steadfastly setting his face towards Jerusalem" (Luke 9 v51), and finally the missionary journeys of Paul and the Gospel being taken to Rome, the heart of the mighty Roman Empire.

In a way my own life has recently seen me undertaking a small pilgrimage within my life long journey of faith. (It seems to be the usual pattern that we all take in our Christian development: small journeys within the larger quest.) My relocation from Leeds to Knutsford after nearly 83 years in that great Yorkshire city, involving long church connections with the same Methodist church, was a *tremendous* step into the unknown, but health issues dictated my decision. My fears were soon allayed through two factors: the nearness of my elder daughter and the warm welcome given me by the local Methodist church. I missed my friends of course but soon felt at home and have enjoyed making new friends.

Celtic Christianity produced a number of pilgrim type missionaries who travelled miles preaching the good news – St Patrick, St Columba, St Aiden, St Cuthbert to name a few. A story from that time tells of one such preacher meeting the king of a Pict tribe. "What will I discover if I give my allegiance to your King Jesus?" the Picts' king asked.

"You will discover wonder upon wonder, and every one of them true!" was the answer he was given.

That story leads me to ask myself a number of questions and I invite you to join in the exercise and ask yourself them too. "What discoveries have we made within our personal faith that would make us recommend to others an allegiance to Jesus? What wonders are there which are worth sharing because they bring to us such meaning and enrichment? What is there within Christian belief and practice that would make the idea of joining a church appealing or at least worth considering?"

Personally I'm still a learner in all this. It's a work in progress. When Jesus said "Be ye therefore perfect" perhaps he was counselling his disciples to "*strive for* perfection." I can't imagine that perfection in this life is achievable but that should not deter us from trying to do our best. It's like the comment I sometimes wrote on pupils' reports: "There is room for improvement." There always is in life and in our faith too but that doesn't prevent us from appreciating the wonders upon wonder to be found in following Jesus.

Here are my thoughts. You will reach your own answers and it would be great if you could share them with me and others some time. I choose three points, three headings, because that's the technique that preachers often use, following the custom of the 4th century Eastern Church Patriarch of Constantinople, St John Chrysostom.

The first heading is MAGIC MOMENTS. You will recognize there the words of a Burt Bacharach song from 1958 with a very catchy whistling introduction. It's a love song : "Magic moments, when two hearts are caring, magic moments, memories we've been sharing. I'll never forget the moment we kissed.. and so on... Times can't erase the memory of these magic moments filled with love."

Those who join the fellowship of Jesus are commiting themselves to a family of love where we sing songs of love in our hymns and where we hear, whenever we worship, his love story. We become part of a love song and a love story. We should therefore expect magic moments and wonder upon wonder. One such consequence is that we begin to see the world through the eyes of Jesus. We recognise its incredible beauty and we learn to love all of God's creatures, great and small, animal and human.

"Let the same mind be in you which was also in Christ Jesus" wrote Paul to the Philippians (2 v.5).

The mind, the attitude of Jesus, was to look at the world and to love what he saw. As we read in the Sermon on the Mount (Matthew 6 v.25-34) for Jesus the splendour of the birds, and the colours of the wild flowers were evidence of a creating, caring God and were signs of his love for each human being. Likewise

Jesus looked at children and at sinful men and women, saw their potential and loved what he saw. That is how he looks at us. We may think we don't deserve such love, but thank God, Jesus thinks we do.

God bombards us with magic moments. It is not a bad idea to lie in bed at the end of each day and before sleep overtakes us to try to recall some of the blessings which have come our way since getting up. They may include a Bible passage which has hit you with a fresh understanding, or a verse of a hymn, a piece of music, a phone call from a friend, a friendly smile and word from the person on the supermarket checkout, a happy, giggling pigtailed little girl skipping by you.

I am not one of those Christians who believes that God engineers our every move, even directing us to an empty space in the carpark. But if you believe in a loving God then you cannot rule out the probability that he will try to get through to you in all sorts of ways and not just in church. Magic moments during Sunday worship we should expect but let us not rule out other times and places. God is not left locked up in this building when the doors are shut and we go home.

The second heading of my "give Christianity a go" challenge is to highlight a further bonus which God gives to believers. This is SACRED SPOTS OR SANCTIFIED SPACES.

Many years ago I bought a Bible in Jerusalem. A friend and I were there on a short leave from National Service in Egypt. It was in Egypt a few months earlier that I had made a commitment to Christ and it seemed appropriate not just to underline a particular verse in Deuteronomy but to write it on the fly leaf of my new Bible which in the days before modern versions appeared was the Authorised King James' edition.

"Thou shalt remember that thou wast a bondman (a slave) in the land of Egypt and the Lord thy God redeemed thee." (15 v.15)

That verse had acquired a personal significance and although Egypt for me was made up of sand, sun, barbed wire, flies and army chores; it had become, and remains, a sanctified space where God had got through to me and changed my life. Over sixty years later I reflect that I have taken on board other sacred spots: churches where I have been privileged to worship and preach many times. For lots of you this building here on the high street in Knutsford will be special as the home where family weddings took place, where your children were christened, where you have said heart wrenching goodbyes to loved ones and given thanks for the departed saints. Here in the weekly programme of worship and events you find fun, inspiration, challenge – and God.

In addition you will have your own sanctified spaces: maybe a favourite rural view point, or a spot where love blossomed or a friendship was cemented; perhaps some place, manmade even, where you stood in awe at the magnificent vista, your breath taken away and a spiritual tingle running down your spine. It could even be your favourite armchair where you relax and think, and drink your tea and where it is easy to offer the odd prayer or two.

The third bonus coming with faith in God is what I shall call UNAWARE ANGELS.

I borrow that phrase from the 12th chapter of the Letter to the Hebrews where the author urges his Christian readers to *practise hospitality*. The Message version of the Bible puts it like this: "Stay on good terms with each other, held together by love. Be ready with a meal or a bed when it's needed. Why some of you have welcomed angels without realising it!"

The Revised Standard Version reads "You may be welcoming angels unaware,"

Angels in the Bible are always messengers – bringing messages from God. In our 21st century we should expect words of challenge and inspiration from modern angels.

One of my favourite hymns is "There's a Light upon the mountains" with the words:

"His angels here are human, not the shining hosts above."

In other words modern angels are ordinary people – unaware that they are being used by God. In such a moment we too may be unaware that in their words or smile God is actually saying something to us. Likewise God sometimes uses us to bring his blessings to others and we too will probably not realise it.

Many years ago we went to a friend's 70th birthday party held at a Christian holiday centre. The celebrations included a short informal service in a large room and I was asked if I would come to the front and say a prayer.

There was a large carpet where the small children were sitting being kept amused with toys. I had to stand amongst them. I was in the middle of the prayer, my eyes closed in concentration, when I felt a tiny hand placed into mine. It was our granddaughter, who was five or six at the time. I don't know why she did it but for me it was a magic moment from an unaware angel making that hall a sacred spot. Perhaps she had felt my nervousness and the message was "Don't worry Grandad. You'll be alright."

Magic moments, sacred spots, unaware angels three bonuses which God in his generosity provides for us. Stay on the lookout for these channels of blessing which sometimes overlap and intertwine. They are ways in which God gets through to us. They are like his Christmas gifts, his birthday presents and his thank you messages all rolled into one – and they are all God's ways of saying to us:

"See how much I really love you!"

They are in fact glimpses of the heaven which Jesus promises to all of us. They are telling us that heaven actually begins on earth.

If you are already a Christian pilgrim then *make progress*. Beware of standing still or going backwards in your faith journey. If you are not yet a pilgrim then don't be put off. Take the risk and test the truth of John Bunyan's hymn that there's no discouragement that will make you relent your first avowed intent to be a pilgrim.

FATHER BROWN
KNOWS BEST

Watching television on a weekday afternoon is a practice which I try to avoid partly because of those depressing adverts targeting the "elderly" such as funeral plans, over 50s insurance and stair lifts! Perhaps many of you feel the same. If however you do tune in during that time slot you will come across a gentle detective series which was first aired in January 2013 and which is the third longest running drama on BBC TV, the first being *Doctors*.

The setting is the mid-1950s in the fictional Cotswold village of Kembleford, where Father Brown, priest at St Mary's Catholic Church, solves murder cases. A bumbling police inspector, who often arrests the wrong suspect, is annoyed by Father Brown's successes. The priest uses the odd remarks of close friends as well as his own wit to solve cases. His clerical vocation gives him an insight into the truth and his commitment to the seal of the Confessional can be helpful through his listening ear and carefully phrased questions. We see all this against the background struggles of a country in the aftermath of the Second World War. The death penalty still stood, which Father Brown of course opposed.

The actor, Mark Williams, ideally portrays the slightly crumpled, mild mannered Roman Catholic Priest whose apparent innocence hides a playful wit and a razor sharp intellect. His greatest strength, both as a priest and as a crime solver, is his understanding and love of individuals. He is not there to judge, but to save souls.

It's a series at least worth looking at and is a pleasant alternative to the majority of television's crime dramas which seem to concentrate on the brutal, the gory, an excessive use of swear words and unnecessary violence.

I give this sermon a title: "Father Brown knows best" but, of course, the insights of Father Brown belong to the author of the stories upon which the TV dramas are based. Can anyone give me his name? Let me give you some information about Gilbert Keith Chesterton. Born in London in 1874, he died at the age of 62 in Beaconsfield, where he is buried in the Roman Catholic Cemetery. That was in June 1936. I was almost six months old so had not got round to reading any of his prolific writings! But during the Covid lockdown period I have tried to dip into his major work, "The Three Apologies." It has been a struggle and I've had to skim many chapters but I have been delighted and inspired by several brilliant purple passages.

Apologies here is not to be thought of as ways of saying sorry. Christian Apologetics is a branch of theology which explains our doctrines to enquiring minds. It is both an explanation and a defence of our faith beliefs. In the early days of Christianity, as the Church was seeking to get organised and accepted as an authentic religion, it had major tasks to face such as the relationship between Christianity and Judaism. Judaism was allowed and tolerated by the Roman Empire. Question marks hung over Christianity though, especially when its breakaway from the covering protection of Judaism became apparent. We see this when Emperor Nero began his savage persecution of Christians around AD 64. By the second century the very existence of the Church was in danger so it became imperative that Apologetics – the defence of the church against its critics – should now widen its scope to explain to the Roman authorities and to the public in general that this new religion was indeed safe and reasonable. The plea was for understanding and acceptance.

The situation produced some great Christian writers and theologians such as Justin Martyr, Irenaeus and Origen, but it was not until the fourth century with the conversion of the Emperor Constantine that the official order came for the cessation of persecution of Christians. Now the Church no longer had to worship and meet in secret. Christianity was recognised as a valid religion and given the full protection of the Roman Law.

The next major use of Christian Apologetics was in the Middle Ages when the rediscovery of the writings of the Greek philosopher Aristotle was arousing interest in the academic world. The Church saw the need to find a place for Reason to be added to their sources of inspiration for belief. According to the training course for Methodist Local Preachers our beliefs have their authority from the Church (Tradition), the Bible, Experience (note the Methodist emphasis) and Reason. These are referred to as "The Building Blocks of our Faith".

The Middle Ages brought the period of Enlightenment, sometimes called the Age of Reason. Its philosophical approach was a considerable threat to Christianity causing many to think about the teachings of the Church and to have doubts. Intellectual giants of theology such as Anselm and Thomas Aquinas came to the defence with their *Arguments* for the existence of God and the role of Jesus. Today's Church is shaped by the turbulence of those times. Church history is fascinating and not irrelevant and boring – as some would claim.

Returning from our (or my) detour I take us back to G.K. Chesterton. In describing his career and achievements Wikipedia uses words such as journalist, art and literary critic, historian, novelist, lay theologian, radio contributor, poet, novelist, playwright and newspaper columnist. He had a towering intellect with a physical frame to match: 6 feet 4 inches and 20 stone 6 pounds. He once commented to his friend George Bernard Shaw, "To look at you George anyone would think a famine had struck England." Shaw retorted, "To look at you, anyone would think that you had caused it." P.G.Wodehouse once described a very loud crash as "a sound like G.K.Chesterton falling onto a sheet of tin." These friendly rivalries suggest that a sense of humour could be added to his qualities.

Here then was a huge man with a large load of fun. Dictionaries of quotations contain lots of his witty comments. Google them and you will find yourself smiling and thinking. The fact that near the end of his life Chesterton was invested by the Pope as *"Knight Commander with Star of the Papal Order of St Gregory the Great"* shows how esteemed he was by the Roman Catholic Church, into which he had transferred his allegiance from the Church of England in his late 40s.

Let's turn now to some of those purple passage pieces from Chesterton's writings which caught my eye during the period of Covid-19 lockdown. It's fascinating really because, although his words were written nearly a hundred years ago, they seem to strike bells for the Church today. Perhaps that shouldn't surprise us because when we think about it the scripture readings that we hear every Sunday in church were not first spoken or written yesterday were they? God's message is not confined by barriers of time but is for ever relevant, new and vital.

The passages which inspired me are from the Third Apology called *The Everlasting Man* written in 1925, especially the chapter *The Strangest Story in the World,* in which the author makes it clear that for him Jesus is *the* unique, eternal Man: God made man, the human and the divine in co-existence, hinted at in John's Gospel though not spelled out until the first great creeds of the early church. Chesterton shared his excitement and refreshing insight at this point when he wrote this:

"The Jesus of the New Testament seems to me to have in a great many ways something superhuman; that is of something human and more than human. A quality running through all his teachings is the persistent idea that he has not come just to teach. If there is one incident which affects me personally as grandly and gloriously human it is that of giving wine at the wedding feast. That is really human in the sense in which a whole crowd of prigs, having the appearance of human beings, can hardly be described as human. Jesus rises superior to all superior persons. "My time has not yet come," is his first response. What does that mean?"

After exploring further the idea of a plan in Jesus's life and mind the author reaches these conclusions:

"From the first to the last the most definite fact is Jesus's knowledge that he is going to die. The story of Christ is the story of a journey – beginning in the paradise of Galilee, gradually climbing into the rising hills of the Mount of Transfiguration, stopping on the way for a discussion or dispute, but with his face set towards the mountain city of Jerusalem."

For present day Christians living a hundred years after Chesterton, his words about the superhuman manhood of Jesus and his journey towards an inevitable and cruel death should cause us to explore deeply the question being asked at the time, "Who is this man?" – especially if our church claims to be Christ centred and Spirit led.

There are other challenges to which these *Three Apologies* point, the most significant one being the overall issue as to how we cope when we are faced with new ideas which we perceive as attacks on our faith and our very existence. (Perhaps even the aftermath of a pandemic).

Chesterton provides hope as he draws his book to a close with a chapter called *The Five Deaths of the Faith*. If that title sounds negative I would want to give it a sub title: *Coping with Change,* but of course I cannot do that.

The 17th century priest and poet John Donne, dean of St Paul's Cathedral, reflecting on the new thinking of the Enlightenment, wrote that "these new philosophies call all in doubt." He thought they were disturbing Christian beliefs and putting out the "fire of zeal", the enthusiasm people had for the Church. Christianity was under attack!

Well it had all happened before with the split from Judaism, then the emergence of heresies mostly about the nature of Jesus – human, divine or both? It has been said that there was not just one Christianity; there were several Christianities with converts having to decide which one to follow.

The relationship with the Roman Empire was a further problem for the Church and periods of severe persecution were endured before that was sorted out. Attempts to destroy this new religion failed, which is rather strange given the power and the ruthlessness of Rome.

The challenges of Reason and Science came much later and were eventually accommodated. More perceived threats were to follow some of which turned out to not be threats, but opportunities. Since then other issues have followed to alarm the Church such as Science versus Religion, and they linger on to this day in debates which can be divisive, creating one side against another in entrenched, opposing and unlistening stances. So we still find evolutionists against creationists, fundamentalists opposed to progressives and in sexual matters the righteous attitude locked in battle with a liberal approach.

We have all been guilty at times of asking the wrong questions and of being unwilling to consider other points of view. We make things worse when we are not prepared to admit that in some of our decisions we could have been mistaken. Why do we find it almost impossible to say "sorry"?

When the enemies of Jesus tried to trap him with trick questions as to whether taxes should be paid to Caesar and also the fate of the woman in the afterlife who, when her husband had died had been married to his brother under the Jewish Religious Law for the protection of widows – and so on through five other brothers (an unlikely scenario), Jesus turned these questions back on them, indicating that they were really missing the point of his message and his mission. In all of our disputes we have to be willing to compromise and to find the middle ground where we can agree on what is essential, otherwise we shall remain for ever at loggerheads. As Archbishop Tutu proved after the

South African Apartheid, reconciliation is the way forward. It is the way of Christ who shows us how to forgive, how to be forgiven and how to live in peace.

As we emerge from the effects of the coronavirus pandemic to face the daunting challenges of post Brexit, Black Lives Matter and the threat of climate change to the environment, we could be forgiven for being flummoxed by our "What happens next?" questions with regard to the world, our country and, for Christians, our church. Where do we go from here? I have to admit my own fears, but recently I have found encouragement and hope from certain sources which I must share with you in closing. One source comes from hymns with two in particular, both by Fred Pratt Green. Their words are these:

"When our confidence is shaken in beliefs
we thought secure, when our spirit in its
sickness seeks but cannot find a cure;
God is active in the tensions of a faith
not yet mature.

God is love; and he redeems us in the Christ
we crucify; this is God's eternal answer
to the world's eternal why; may we in this
faith maturing be content to live and die!"

In the other hymn we sing:

"The Church of Christ, in every age
beset by change but Spirit-led,
must claim and test its heritage
and keep on rising from the dead.

Another source of hope for me and for all of us must be of course the words of Jesus and especially in our context the promise given to Peter and the disciples: "On this rock I will build my church, and the gates of hell will not prevail against it."(Matthew 16v18)

The final encouragement came from G.K.Chesterton responding to those who thought that the Church was on its last legs. People were saying that the Church had had its day and was terminally ill. Christianity was finished. "Not so!" was Chesterton's vigorous opinion, pointing to the fact that over the centuries Christendom has had a series of revolutions and in each one of them Christianity has died many times but has risen again for it has a God who knows his way out of the grave. He concludes with what he refers to as an extraordinary fact that Europe has been turned upside down over and over again and at the end of these revolutions the same religion has again been found on top. The Faith of the Church is always converting the age, emerging not as an old religion but as a new religion, transformed and transforming. "Heaven and earth will pass away but my words will not pass away." So said Jesus. That promise has been fulfilled whenever the Church has been in an end of life crisis.

As the hymn says the Church of Christ in every age must keep on rising from the dead. When all is said and done, (my apologies for the jargon and more so for all the words *I* have said this morning – too many I guess), I have to conclude that Father Brown , or G.K.Chesterton, knows best and so does Jesus and so do all you optimistic, hope filled Christians. Who am

I to disagree with such faith, such trust, such courage, such love?

There is an old story that when Jesus arrived back in Heaven on Ascension Day the angels asked "What have you done to ensure that the Gospel message will not die?" Jesus told them that he had left things in the hands of his disciples. "But what if they fail?" the incredulous angels ask. Jesus answered, "I am depending on them." A legend of course but, I wonder, is Jesus equally relying on his 21st century disciples (that is us) in our crisis situation?

Now a moment for quiet reflection.

Let us pray:

Lord, in our lonely hours,
and when our spirit faints,
we are encouraged by your life,
and by your saints.

If we've no breath for praise,
no thoughts to frame a prayer,
we know you need no words of ours
to prompt your care.

If in excess of pain,
or grief, we stammer why?
It comforts us that on your cross
This was your cry.

Yet, in serenest faith,
transforming Calvary,
you trusted in the Father's love –
and so must we.

AMEN

BE YE THEREFORE PERFECT

Some Bible passages and verses are difficult to understand because they contradict our personal ideas of what God is like.

Even among the vast number of wise things that Jesus said we come across a few such "hard sayings" (as they are called) which make us pause and ponder, "Did Jesus really say that and if so what does it mean?"

One such verse is in the Sermon on the Mount, which is a summary of his advice to his disciples, both then and now. It is our Christian Manifesto. It's in Matthew chapters 5 to 8. Read it often. Follow its teaching as best you can.

The verse is Matthew 5 v.48:

"Be ye therefore perfect,
even as your Father in heaven is perfect."

Our first impression is that Jesus gave his disciples (and therefore us) an impossible task.

The verse I have just read is from the King James or Authorised Version – the Bible on which I and the older folk here cut our teeth. Published in 1611 it has the language of Shakespeare's day with its *Thees* and *Thous* and rich poetic prose and eloquence.

It was the only Bible we had in church, school and home. Our horizons were not widened until the 1960s when translators started to produce Bibles in up to date modern English, easy to read and to understand.

There was resistance of course, especially from within the church. We have a tendency to produce the odd head in the sand Christian who wants to preserve the status quo – maybe because they are afraid of stepping out in faith.

Thus the alleged comment of one objector to the New English Bible of 1961 that, "If the Authorised Version was good enough for St Paul then it's good enough for me!" displays an ignorance of church history and of Bible translations.

Try googling the story of how we got our Bible and its translations into English, and you will be amazed, as I was, at the sheer volume of work that has gone on – and still is happening.

"Be ye therefore perfect" is from the Authorised Version. That could be the first clue in our search for what Jesus meant.

If taken at face value and as an order, where is the encouragement?

Jesus raises us up, he never puts us down.

But if perfection is out of reach…?

In our desperation we need to look at modern translations. The New English Bible tells us "There must be no limit to your Goodness".

This seems to me to be making progress, but the popular Good News Bible takes us back to "You must be perfect".

The new International Version sticks with "Be perfect, therefore, as your heavenly Father is perfect."

Lots of people find inspiration in The Message version. So do I but we must remember that it is not a translation. It is a paraphrase, putting the bible into the sort of everyday language that we all use in conversation.

The American author, rather than a committee of scholars as with the other examples I have quoted, produced *this* for his readers;

> *"In a word* (said Jesus) *what I'm saying is Grow Up. You are kingdom subjects. Now live like it. Live out your God-created identity. Live generously and graciously toward others, the way God lives toward you"*

Strangely I find it easier to imagine Jesus talking to his disciples in *this* way rather than in committee-speak terms.

"Be ye therefore perfect" or "Live generously and graciously towards others"

Which version sits more easily with you?

But let's move on to consider what are the implications for us if we attempt to carry out this instruction of Jesus – once we have worked out what it means in our 21st century context.

When I was a boy, about 6 or 7, for a time I had a small diary. At that age I didn't write much in it but I had some coloured pencils. (Perhaps they had all appeared in my Christmas Stocking). At the end of each day I scribbled in the space with the colour which summed up my behaviour during that day – from gold to green to red to black. You get the idea. I seem to remember that there were quite a few black, bad-boy days and not many gold perfect days. Perhaps here was the dawning of personal conscience when we begin to recognise for ourselves what is right behaviour and what is wrong.

Then there was Miss Verity. My sister, who was three years older, went to the same school and Miss Verity was her class teacher. From what she had said I was a bit scared of Miss Verity and therefore was a little perturbed when I was sent to her classroom one day with some message, I don't remember what.

The class was working quietly in their exercise books, having just been set an essay, or what in those days was called a composition.

Presumably they had all copied neatly the sentence written at the top of the board, which Miss Verity insisted should start each new piece of work.

"Only the best is good enough".

Looking at the state of my handwriting today, I reflect that perhaps I ought to have had Miss Verity as my teacher!

Before being sent back to my own classroom she did ask me to write a word on the board and for the class to watch. Somebody must have told her I was good at spelling. The word was "beautiful".

Thankfully I got it right.

It was also a lesson in self-confidence because I was a very shy boy, terrified of teachers – but no longer of Miss Verity. Over the years I've not changed much (ha ha) – and my sister's writing is still better than mine.

It's strange how little incidents from early school days stick with us. I remember my very first teacher, Miss Brown. She was wonderful, perfect. At Christmas we had our little post box and made cards to send to each other. Miss Brown let me be the postman! Ah! She was great.

We had a teacher called Sally Hutton who was an aunt of the great Yorkshire batsman and England captain Len Hutton, one of my childhood heroes. A bit eccentric she would go behind the blackboard in the middle of a lesson. We speculated as to why and concluded that she was changing her false teeth. In the playground we used to make fun and chanted:

"Sally Hutton, leg of mutton, pork, beef, chops"

I must mention Mr Hirst, the woodwork teacher. I didn't like him because if you produced a poor joint he would hit you over the head with part of your work. His lessons often gave me a headache! And my woodworking skills certainly did not improve.

Going back to that command of Jesus to be perfect, I seemed to have reached a dead end in my thinking – a contradiction that here Jesus didn't mean what he said.

So I did something which I haven't done for years. I had a look at my book of John Wesley's sermons – forty four of them which the founder of Methodism had first published in 1746 for the guidance of his preachers, and which Methodist preachers ever since have been required to read during their training because they cover all our main beliefs and practices. There it was – Sermon 35 entitled "Christian Perfection"

The sermon is based on Philippians 3 verse 12 with Paul's words:

"Not as though I had already attained perfection or were already perfect."

Wesley's opening opinion is that there is scarcely any other idea in the whole of scripture that has given greater offence and that anyone who preaches that perfection is attainable in this life is in danger of being regarded as a heathen.

But as Jesus himself uses the expression John Wesley has to very carefully (and methodically of course) explain in what sense Christians are not perfect and in what sense Christians may claim perfection.

Wesley points out the obvious:

*Christians are not perfect in the knowledge of
God's ways though they trust in God's love
and seek his guidance.
They are not perfect in their behaviour.
They do not always set a good example.
They are often slow to understand God's ways,
prone to misinterpreting the scriptures.*

Wesley suggests that there are a thousand other defects in conversation and behaviour to which Christians might succumb. In this life we are never totally free from temptation.

He concludes that Christian Perfection is a further term for Holiness. Scriptural Holiness is another of Wesley's emphases, embraced by Methodism as part of the very core of our beliefs and practices, not confined to us of course but welcomed by other Christian denominations.

Perhaps to add weight to his sermon on Christian Perfection John Wesley published at the end his brother Charles's hymn "God of all power, and truth, and grace" – all 28 verses! Our current hymn book has reduced that to six. Essentially it is our personal prayer that God will "perfect holiness in me".

"Give me a new, a perfect heart,
Free from all doubt and fear at last;
the mind which was in Christ impart,
and let my spirit hold you fast.

Now let me gain perfection's height…"

Christian Perfection then: just one of the many Methodist emphases embodied in our hymn book.

That's why it is called *"Singing the Faith"* because that's what we do and that's why during the Covid crisis many of us have felt so deprived.

In Wesley's sermon instructions are set down on the conduct of Methodists then and still today but not only that, for we are given Wesley's insights into the nature of God.

He is not a stifling, unforgiving God like my woodwork teacher, bashing us when we don't get things right.

Neither is he like Miss Hutton occasionally showing no interest in us, (though sometimes it may seem like that.)

He is more like Miss Brown who gives us the freedom to grow and enjoy life, to join in his games – or like Miss Verity who gives us the courage to believe in ourselves and to develop our God given talents to the best of our ability and learning from our mistakes.

"Be ye therefore perfect" does make sense as long as we see it as advice to live generously towards others.

And that is up to us, with a bit of help from the Holy Spirit.

In the week that lies before us, as we continue to strive for perfection, may we enjoy a perfect week – not that we'll achieve it but in the sense of the old school report comment "Tries hard but has not yet reached his/her full potential".

If God were our teacher I feel he may look at us with a loving smile of approval, tongue in cheek.

That is real encouragement – and sufficient blessing.

PRAYER MATTERS

"More things are wrought by prayer than this world dreams"

So wrote the 19th century poet Alfred Tennyson. In other words the power and the effect of prayer cannot be measured by human beings.

In this service I want us to examine the practice of prayer.

Why do we do it?

How do we do it?

Is there any point in it, or is it just a misguided waste of time?

Everybody knows what it is to pray because we have all done it when younger and maybe still do it, especially at times of crisis in our lives; yes, even those who do not believe in God may be moved to utter an appeal to the God they don't believe in.

So what is it all about, this business of prayer? I have no definitive answers to offer, no proofs to give. I can only point our thinking in certain directions hopefully leading to further consideration and discussion, maybe even to the stage of experimentation in our journey into the practice, art and skills of praying.

I have given this sermon the title of "Prayer Matters." That can be interpreted in two ways.

It can mean anything to do with matters of prayer, such as examples of prayer, opinions on prayer by poets, clerics, theologians or anyone.

Or it can be a statement affirming that prayer is really, really important. It matters and should not be ignored or neglected. Prayer is powerful and crucial to our world.

Our thinking today will cover both these areas and could lead us to the latter conclusion that prayer is *really* important.

Our starting point is Nehemiah and the reading is from Nehemiah chapter 2:

Nehemiah 2 v.1-8

This little story and the character of Nehemiah belong to the period right at the very end of the recorded history of Old Testament Judaism. We are in what is known as the Inter-Testamental Era just before the arrival of Jesus and the Christian New Testament.

The first chapter of Nehemiah sets the scene and is your reading for this afternoon's homework!

In it you will see that the exiled Jews are eager to return to their own country from which their parents and grandparents had been banished when Jerusalem had been flattened at least 70 years before.

Since then, in the face of persecution, dispersed Jews all over the world have worked hard in and for their adopted land and done very well – being held together by their faith in God and family loyalties.

The pattern continues to this day with the diaspora of Jews far exceeding the number of Jews in the State of Israel.

Nehemiah was one such person. If you read the first chapter you will gather that he has risen to a rank of high authority in the court of the Emperor himself, King Artaxerxes. He was even authorised to represent the Empire – to be an ambassador to foreign countries. He had the eyes and ears of the Emperor and one of his jobs, he tells us, was to be a cupbearer to Artaxerxes.

The task of a cupbearer gave him regular access to the man in total power. A real privilege but it could be fraught with danger (as Donald Trump's closest aides discovered.)

As cupbearer you would be required to take the first sip of wine to check that it was not poisoned. You would always try to look cheerful. We don't like to be served by sourpuss waiters do we?

An Emperor could remove your glum looks by removing your head.

In one sense things have not changed much.

Trump used character assassination to destroy his perceived enemies which is equally, if not more, cruel.

Nehemiah cannot help looking downcast at the bad news he had received of how fellow Jews in Jerusalem were suffering.

The perceptive king notices his cupbearer's gloom and asks what is wrong.

Nehemiah pours out his people's plight.

"What are you requesting?" asks the king.

Observe the response.

Still very much afraid Nehemiah tells us "I prayed to the God of Heaven" and immediately asks for permission to visit Jerusalem, to oversee its rebuilding This is an arrow prayer – what the hymn writer describes when he writes:

"Prayer is the soul's sincere desire,
uttered or unexpressed"

I often think that our prayers both personal and communal are too wordy.

Did not Jesus warn his followers that those who heap up empty phrases will not be heard just because of their many words?:

"Your Father knows what you need before you ask him"(Matthew 6 v.8)

No need (or time) for Nehemiah to pause for thought. God knew the situation and God reached out to *him*. We can treasure that idea as we recognise the value of arrow prayers.

But let's move on.

We listen to a reading from Matthew 6 v.1-15

Matthew 6 v.1-15 (NRSV)

Most of our prayers will be personal – just you and God, and are therefore secret and God who sees in secret will reward us by listening. This is his promise.

Let's think about secret prayers. Some of those will be familiar so in this passage we come across the Lord's Prayer – taught by the Lord, Jesus, but intended to be the Disciples' Prayer, your prayer and my prayer.

"This is how I want you to pray," Jesus tells us.

Maybe there is no other command in the whole

of history which has been so obeyed. At this very moment those memorable phrases will be on the lips of many petitioners. Our world is soaked in the Lord's or the Disciples' Prayer. If I were to preach solely on The Lord's Prayer I could find something to say for every Sunday in the year without exhausting all its possibilities.

We sometimes sing:

O what peace we often forfeit,
O what needless pain we bear,
All because we do not carry
Everything to God in prayer!

A plea there that our prayers be regular (daily even), not just once in a while or once a week in church.

Another hymn says that "prayer is the Christian's vital breath" and we know what happens when our breathing gets restricted.

Regular praying will lead to a recognised pattern:

prayers for family and friends;

prayers of thanksgiving and confession and within all those, prayers which we have learned to love and to treasure, such as the Lord's Prayer;

There will be other prayers which we have claimed for ourselves because we can pray them and mean every word.

At this point I feel I am in a similar position to the theologian Alister McGrath when he writes about the sacraments in his book "The Landscape of Faith".

He admits that he has not been able to deal with such a vast subject adequately in a brief space and decided that his best course of action was for him to set out some approaches which have helped him personally, whilst making it clear that there is much more to be said.

If I were a Local Preacher in training handing this my sermon script to a tutor for assessment I would be asked all sorts of questions about structure, where is it going, what are my sources of authority?

The answer that the subject is too big and I can only share my own experience, may not be well received but that's my only defence.

I leave you to judge.

I go on then to share with you some of my favourite sources of inspiration in addition of course to the Bible (always the first priority) and the Hymn Book.

I like short pithy prayers often appearing in books of quotations.

They get attributed to different people, and we cannot be certain which is correct.

Whether or not John Wesley prayed these words cannot be proved.

But they appeal to me:

"Lord, let me not live to be useless."

How about this?

"Lord, in my busy day, if I forget thee do not thou forget me." (We all know the stress of busy days!)

I love to dip into the ancient prayers of the Church of England, perhaps because of my time as an Anglican choirboy. The words of the General Thanksgiving mean a lot to me. Somewhere I have a sermon devoted to it.

A prayer of St Ignatius is lodged in my memory. I put the words into modern English:

"Teach us good Lord to serve you as you deserve: to give and not to count the cost, to fight and not to heed the wounds; to toil and not to seek for rest; to labour and not to ask for any reward except that of knowing that we do your will."

And the prayer for the second Sunday in Advent from the Book of Common Prayer resonates for me with its memorable request that on hearing the words of scripture we should read, mark, learn and inwardly digest them.

Before I round off my thoughts on prayer there is one more area which I want to touch on because it is important and we take it for granted. We pray for others and forget that people pray for us, for all sorts of reasons.

St Paul opens his letter to his Christian friends in Philippi with the words:

"I thank my God every time I remember you, constantly praying with joy in every one of my prayers for all of you" (Philippians 1 v.3)

Prayer for others is part of our Christian ministry. Have you ever been in a situation where the prayers of others have carried you through a crisis?

In the late summer of 2016 I lay on a hospital bed in Leeds following a twisted bowel operation.

For eleven days I was unable to eat.

Tubes blocked my throat.

The food trolley passed by several times each day. A glance was given me and a smile before they moved on (not that I was hungry anyway!) It is one way to lose weight but not recommended. I was helpless and can only conclude that the grace of God and the prayers of friends and family came to my rescue.

Never under-estimate the power of praying for others – and do not be too shy to let them know that they are in your prayers.

I leave you with the challenge to think about prayer, to experiment, to persevere, to be excited, not afraid.

You may discover that there is truth in the words of William Law, an 18th century English clergyman, that "the one who has learned to pray has learned the greatest secret of a happy life."

Which brings us back to our starting point that "More things are wrought by prayer than this world dreams".

CVs

How many of you, I wonder, have your own CV? Nothing to do with corona virus, (thankfully!)

Nor is it the latest model of a French manufacturer's car.

The CV I refer to is from the Latin Curriculum Vitae.

It is a written record of your education and the jobs you have done which you will send when applying for a post. It may also include your life outside work such as your interests, hobbies, courses attended and so on. "It will look good on your CV," is advice given to young people by parents and teachers.

The process is followed even within the Methodist ministry. There may have been changes since I was a Circuit Steward in the Leeds West Circuit over twenty years ago when we were looking for a new minister. I hope so because I well remember the challenges and the stress of the task. Then, and maybe still, just before a minister was due to move to another Circuit she or he had to submit a profile for publication in a book of profiles sent out to Circuit Stewards engaged in the task of recommending a suitable minister for their vacancy. At an appointed hour the fun of the head hunt began with scores of phone calls and endless frustrations and further searches through the Yellow Book of profiles. Ministers too would be perhaps be waiting by their phone with their book of Circuit Profiles wondering "Will I fit into their set up?"

We Methodists call this "Stationing" for some reason. An odd name but if you have ever found yourself in the chaos of a London Railway terminal at rush hour then maybe you could draw some parallels. Thankfully it only comes round every few years.

Like our new minister I too have recently made a pilgrimage across the Pennines to Knutsford. Thankfully I join you as a worshipper and did not have to submit a CV – otherwise you might have sent back the message "Stay where you are!"

But seeing that I come as a Local Preacher willing to serve when and where possible what if you had wanted to know a bit about me before you accepted me in that role? What would you make of me if the important bit of my profile about my beliefs read as follows:

I see the Bible as a book about fighting oppression, about a God who isn't neutral but who is a biased God, biased in favour of the weak, the oppressed, the down-trodden and the despised.

People are beautiful, I believe, because each is made in the image of God, and therefore to hate, imprison or discriminate is like spitting in the face of God. To degrade the dignity of God is blasphemy so wherever this happens the people of God must claim it back, and free the injured.

Therefore I will speak out against injustices and will be outspoken on issues between Israel and Palestine, climate change, poverty, cooperation amongst the world's Faiths (God is not a Christian), women's rights, the acceptance of the LGBTQ+ community. (I would not worship a homophobic God.)

I have a mischievous sense of humour. In one of my talks in church I told a joke about Mary and Joseph getting to the stable. Joseph bangs on the door of the inn and asks; "Please, please let us in, my wife is pregnant." "That's not my fault," says the inn keeper. "And it's not mine either," says Joseph.

If you were on a selection committee I wonder how you would respond to my CV. Would it be a thumbs up vote or a thumbs down?

I need to confess that I have tricked you because actually that is *not* my CV though I agree with the sentiments being expressed. I did qualify my introduction to it with the words "If my CV read like this…." Well it doesn't!

If you turn to a book of sermons called "By way of the Heart" by Mark Oakley, Dean of St John's College, Cambridge and find the sermon titled "A Saint for our Day" (p98) you will discover whose words these are. Some of you may already have guessed. And should you object to them then you are disagreeing with none other than the former Archbishop of Capetown and courageous opponent of the repressive system of apartheid, Desmond Tutu.

Even the joke about Joseph and the inn keeper belong to him.

Apparently, after he had told it he started to giggle and then shriek and belly-laugh with tears running down his cheeks. His is an infectious laughter, encouraging people to join in the fun and the joy of following Jesus.

Nelson Mandela described Tutu as "sometimes strident, often tender, never afraid and seldom without humour." Given such qualities, and for all his work heading the post-Apartheid Peace and Reconciliation Group in South Africa, it is not surprising that he was awarded the Nobel Peace Prize.

I for one would not want to alter my CV if it corresponded with Desmond Tutu's beliefs. Would you?

Mark Oakley's sermon, which I acknowledge I have used, is called "A Saint for our Day." An apt description of a remarkable person.

In our current world crises perhaps one of our most urgent of tasks is to pray that God will raise up more such "Saints for our Day."

There seems to be a distinct shortage of them.

"Please God, give us more saints for our day.
And grant us the courage to give them
our full support. Amen."

ADVICE FOR PREACHERS, NEW AND EXPERIENCED

A few years ago, (2003 to be precise), I had the enormous privilege of preaching the sermon at a Service of Recognition of a Methodist Local Preacher. The invitation had come from Jill, who had been a member of the training class which I ran in the Leeds West Circuit, where I was the Circuit Tutor.

Jill's husband, our Circuit Superintendent, became in charge of the Skipton Circuit so Jill did the final stages of her training there.

The Recognition Service was on a Sunday evening at the village chapel in Hetton – a fairly large box shaped building which was full.

I had learned that this was the place of worship of the leading lady and her husband featured in the film, "The Calendar Girls." She wasn't at the service because of a family Christening that morning but plenty of people were and they were all fully clothed and respectable. Even the preacher had been instructed to wear his gown with the trimmings.

I preached on a verse from the Letter to the Ephesians and, with a little help from the "Star Trek" films, arrived at the message that the task of the preacher is to "boldly go and proclaim the Gospel."

Reflecting back I conclude that I didn't do a very good job with that sermon. It was too long, too theological and too serious. If I were to have the honour of preaching on such an occasion again I would tackle it differently.

"But you don't need a Recognition Service to try to suggest advice to preachers do you? You can humbly offer to share some of the lessons you have picked up in a long career of over sixty years of trying to proclaim the gospel." That's what I told myself and that's why I hesitatingly share this sermon with its somewhat uninspiring title "Advice to preachers, new and experienced"

There are three parts (or bullet points), because that's what preachers often do and that's how listeners are helped to remember the message. In summary they are these:

1.   *Preach with confidence*
2.   *Preach with courage*
3.   *When preaching be ever conscious of your own inadequacies.*

Let's examine these sections in turn starting with the first bit of advice:

1.   *Preach with confidence in your calling*

When would be preachers are asked to give an account of their call to preach to their Circuit Local Preachers Meeting (it's part of their course), invariably they describe their initial reluctance to respond positively.

They do not consider themselves good enough or worthy to undertake such a high calling.

So delaying tactics are used before a definite commitment can be made.

In my own case I felt the urge to preach around 1957 but it was not until 1961 that I joined the preachers' training scheme, and 1962 when I was recognised.

By that time, as a member of our Circuit Mission Band, and then being let loose on trial, as we quaintly still call it, I had quite a few services and sermons in my locker. But I had a lot to learn, and still have.

We should not be alarmed by these gaps nor by the rigours of training. The delay is perfectly natural to many preachers. Indeed it is almost predicted in the call of the prophets. Think of Isaiah's response to God:

"Not me Lord. I'm not good enough (a man of unclean lips…)*"*

Think of Jeremiah: "I'm only a youth!"

Before them Moses, the greatest of all Jewish prophets:

"Surely not me Lord. I stammer. My brother Aaron is a much better speaker."

"Here am I, send me," does not come easily.

Most preachers began with their excuses. It takes time (maybe years) before the positive commitment can be made to accept the calling and then to persevere.

In a way a Recognition Service is a bit like a wedding ceremony. The couple make their vows, they enjoy their moment recognising that this is not an ending it's a beginning and an exciting learning curve has started.

You know that you are married.

Sadly of course it doesn't always work out.

Preachers *know* that they have been called to great task, so in spite of wobbles along the way they can be confident of their calling by God and of their commitment to Him.

This is real. It has not been done lightly. Preach with confidence in your calling.

2. Preach with courage and belief in your message

Sometimes, of course, we get it wrong or our theological understanding changes. Recently I've had a clear out of many of my old sermons.

Looking through them I realise that my views alter over the years – and so they should as we read and study.

Lots of people in our services and certainly those who have rejected the Church still have ideas about God which they picked up in Sunday School many years ago.

Scholarship has moved on. My lovely atheist friends have some very strange and outdated notions about God and of what we believe.

Richard Dawkins and company seem to think that we have not progressed from Victorian times and accuse us of being anti-science, of denying evolution, of clinging to a literal belief in Adam and Eve, and similar myths, of seeing God as a punishing disciplinarian whose rules are in the Bible which, being the word of God, cannot be questioned.

A few Christians may be like that but many accept modern scholarship as taught in our colleges and universities.

Christianity is all about change. Encourage your congregations to think about these challenges and not to get stuck in the past.

Say you have prepared a sermon which God has laid on your heart. Preach it with courage, even though parts of it may leave you with as yet unclear conviction.

Soon after I had arrived in Knutsford our minister, Rob Cotton, invited me to share a service with him by preaching the sermon.

My current one at the time had the title "Everybody needs good Neighbours".

I had my misgivings making me wonder whether I should stick with that.

Knutsford is a very different place from inner city Leeds where we were surrounded by mixed racial and religious groupings as well as poverty, unemployment and food banks.

But maybe my new neighbours needed to hear this not only to learn from whence I was coming, but also to appreciate some of the differences between a city circuit and a fairly comfortable market town set up.

So I went ahead, a bit fearful of what their response would be.

At the end of the service, whilst I was thanking the organist and making my way to the door to shake hands with the worshippers, I was challenged by one young man who thanked me for some good points I had made but went on to reel off a number of theological errors in my sermon. I looked for him afterwards so that we could discuss these "errors" but by the time I had talked to people he had gone. Thankfully all the other comments were favourable and I was pleased to discover that there were some folk who shared my sometimes radical views, and read the same books.

So then always try to preach your message with courage.

Challenge your hearers to thought and action.

If there are contentious and unpopular things let them be said in love.

Accept praise with care and criticism with grace bearing in mind always that you may have to consider what you have said – maybe to think again.

Which leads me into a third and final point:

3. *As a preacher, be ever conscious of your own inadequacies.*

I remember some advice given to me years ago by an experienced preacher:

*"Always preach to your congregation,
never preach at them"*

To that I would add: When you preach, preach to yourself. The message is not just for them.

It's also for me.

Another bit of advice picked up from long ago was this:

> *"Never start a sermon with the personal pronoun I "; advice which I have followed very strictly.*

The sermon is not about me. We point congregations to God through our Saviour, Jesus. Like the writer to the Hebrews our message is "Fix your eyes on Jesus."

I sometimes think that our evangelical emphasis on personal salvation can lead us off track. Remember that the prayer which Jesus taught begins with *Our Father* not *My Father*.

My church in Leeds decided to buy an extra hymn book, *Songs of Fellowship*.

Looking through the index one day I made some interesting discoveries.

Over 200 of the 1690 songs began with the personal pronoun *I* whereas only 79 started with *Jesus*.

Our regular Hymns and Psalms on the other hand, had 823 hymns of which only 18 started with *I* but 45 began with *Jesus*.

I haven't had a detailed look at *Singing the Faith* yet but Jesus appears to be narrowly in the lead. As this new hymn book includes a number of worship songs this accounts for the change of balance.

I would urge you though to take time and care when choosing your hymns. They enrich the whole service.

Oh and don't neglect our great Charles Wesley hymns. Through our hymns we really are singing our faith.

In conclusion I direct you to Charles Wesley's words in the hymn "Behold the servant of the Lord (546 StF) with its lovely tune Mozart:

> *"Behold the servant of the Lord!*
> *I wait thy guiding eye to feel,*
> *to hear and keep thy every word,*
> *to prove and do thy perfect will*
> *joyful from my own works to cease,*
> *glad to fulfil all righteousness."*

(Note the humility of the hymn writer and apply that to your role as a preacher.) Continue in the same vein:

> *"Me if thy grace vouchsafe to use,*
> *meanest of all thy creatures, me,*
> *the deed, the time, the manner choose;*
> *let all my fruit be found of thee…"*

> *"Meanest of all thy creatures.."* Who indeed are we that God has chosen us to proclaim his word?

But chosen us he has, in spite of our unworthiness: therefore, let us proceed to our pulpits to proclaim the Gospel with confidence in our calling, courageous in our message and, with a large measure of humility, ever conscious of our own inadequacies.

Please pray with me the last two verses of that Charles Wesley hymn:

"My every weak though good design
o'errule or change, as seems thee meet;
Jesus, let all my work be thine!
Thy work, O Lord, is all complete,
and pleasing in thy Father's sight;
thou only hast done all things right.
Here then to thee thine own I leave;
mould as thou wilt thy passive clay;
but let me all thy stamp receive,
but let me all thy words obey,
serve with a single heart and eye,
and to thy glory live and die."

Amen